Redemption Value

by

Gary Beck

To the memory of A.D., a bright talent,
never realized, gone too soon.

Contents

Social Adaptation

In the 1950's
when a girl dumped a boy
he listened to sad songs,
forgot her by and by.

In the 1960's
when a girl dumped a boy
he smoked pot,
protested the war.

In the 1970's and '80's
when a girl dumped a boy
he got drunk,
demanded his ring.

In the 1990's
when a girl dumped a boy
he stalked her,
sometimes attacked her.

If the trend continues
of violent resentment
when a girl dumps a boy….

Pre-Boarding

I come closer each day
to the end of my journey
and am still weighed down
with excess baggage,
despite having renounced
caviar, fine wine, Warhols,
but cannot yet give up
books I cherish,
though I still can't determine
their value in the scheme of things.
Fortunately,
ego has diminished,
so if I'm cremated
my books won't burn with me,
if I'm interred
they won't molder with me,
and I've almost stopped worrying
about who I'll leave them to.

Unregulated Emissions

The Information Age
will soon be replaced
by the Explanation Age,
conducted by the media
bringing in diverse experts
who explain everything
to a vulnerable public
desperate to understand
what's happening to us,
economic collapse,
natural disasters,
man-made disasters,
that continue to get worse,
despite our being told
by well-fed politicians
things will get better.

Desertion

Leisure time was once the goal
of middle-class America,
vacations of sun and fun,
adult recreation,
parties at the club, tennis,
while their children of neglect
discovered alcohol,
marijuana, teen sex,
anti-social attitudes.
Parents didn't bother
with behavior instruction,
so children of neglect
were held responsible
for what they did wrong,
with no mitigation
despite having to learn
how to do things on their own.

Measure

Time ticks away
faster and faster
as I age,
hurrying me
inevitably
to finality

Values

A man passed me on the street
on a cold winter day
wearing a stained Met's jacket,
torn army cami pants,
an expression of despair,
a forgotten veteran
consigned to homelessness
after serving in a foreign land,
then returning to a foreign land
where he was no longer needed,
cast out by those he protected.

A woman passed me on the street
on a cold winter day
wearing a mink coat and hat,
exotic rhino-hide boots,
an expression of despair
since her pampered tea cup dog
didn't seem to appreciate
the doggie mink coat,
diamond earrings, pearl necklace
that she went through so much trouble
to get for her ungrateful pet.

Worker's Dilemma

The strident demand
of master alarm clock
yanks me untimely
from wistful dream,
curse, shut it off,
doze off again,
then burst awake,
overslept,
shower, shave, dress,
rush to work,
late again.
The implacable
office manager eye
glistens tyrannically,
glares accusingly
sending me to my computer
afraid of confrontation,
as long as I'm dependent
on my meager salary.

Policy Factions

The issues of our time
are seldom what they seem
as we sanction countries
for developing nuclear weapons,
yet sanctions never stop
development of nuclear weapons,
only hurt ordinary folk,
since the wealthy and powerful
remain comfortable, well-fed,
secure in their positions,
never deterred
by economic pressure
to change their ways,
an American fantasy
that the people will revolt,
replace their leadership
with democracy,
a political delusion
common in the U.S.A.,
where we want everyone to love us,
despite the mess we made
in Iraq, Afghanistan,
in ill chosen invasions
that changed nothing for the better
at a prodigious cost
in national treasure,
our young men and women
volunteers trusting their country
not to expend their lives

without good reason,
and we gave them wounds and death,
then withdrew our troops,
another failed venture
that weakened us at home, abroad,
while all the lands that hated us
gloated at our defeat,
calculating how to harm us
as we cowered at home
in a crippled economy
overseen by a selfish congress
enrapt with its own agenda,
apparently unconcerned
that many Americans
may fall off a fiscal cliff,
the people's suffering preferred

to distressing their masters,
whose comforts come before
the needs of the nation..

Dark Days

Another rampage
slaughtering children
in a horrific attack
blighting America
in what has become
a regular event,
the weekly detonation
of a disturbed man
inflicting his madness
on helpless victims,
for real or imagined
obsessive grievances,
always concluding
with homicide
then suicide.

Revenge

The rain falls steadily,
acid eating away
levels of protection
insufficient to deter
chemical attack,
nature's payback
for environmental abuse.

Exertion

The open air café is closed now.
Customers who lingered all day
nursing a cup of coffee,
may or may not miss
watching people pass by,
observing the oddities,
the proud beauty strutting,
the young prince of the city
ambitions not yet defeated,
an abundance of obesity,
most of all, faces of fear
dissolving from constant stress
in the never ending effort
to subsist in trying times.

The System

The democrats claim
they support the people.
The republicans strive
to sustain the wealthy.
Somehow, America,
a nation in need,
always takes second place
to various agendas
proposed by those
seeking re-election,
remarkably similar,
regardless of
political parties,
requiring money
for their campaigns
that usually comes
from the same contributors,
investment insuring
cooperative employees.

Heroes

I read the Times in the morning,
watch tv news each day,
a few magazines, Foreign Affairs,
may be slightly better informed
than the average citizen,
have been doing this a long time,
yet still cannot understand
how so many remain good
in a world of seething evil.
I know without enough good
hope will be extinguished,
and cannot help admire
warriors of goodness
who preserve the light
always under assault.

Make Haste

The city bulges with people
rushing to work, sleep, play,
in an energetic jostle
that leads to destination,
concerts, shows, museums,
the endless entertainment
of a great metropolis
deluding the middle class
they can escape the limits
 of class distinctions.

Cost of Living

The nation is beleaguered
in an economic crisis,
with elected officials
squabbling over spending
as if it were their money,
not the income from the people.
Our enormous public debt,
as well as huge expenditures
jeopardizes stability,
fading hopes of recovery,
yet the Pentagon
gets hundreds of billions,
wastes billions yearly
without making restitution
to the taxpayers,
so some of us conclude
our children won't go to college
as we pay for the F35.

Momentous Event

A speeding car jumped the curb,
hit a woman walking down the street.
People rushed to the scene
some to help, most to gawk.
Many deployed camera phones
eager to capture disaster, suffering.
Someone called 911.
Soon sirens were heard
attracting larger crowds.
Emergency services arrived,
placed the woman on a stretcher,
loaded her in an ambulance,
raced off, intent on life saving.
The police questioned the driver
obviously distressed by the crash.
He asked over and over:
"How is she? How is she?"
The police ignored his questions,
tested him for alcohol
then took him into custody,
two lives dramatically changed
in one disastrous moment.

Equalizer

The wealthy drink champagne,
exclusive bottled water,
consuming the best
money can buy,
living beyond the means
of ordinary folk,
convinced they are better
by accumulating more
than the rest of us.
Somehow they've forgotten,
despite all their possessions.
we all breath the same air,
a rude reminder
of equality.

Second Hand

The older we get
the faster time passes,
meaningless to those
with empty lives,
no opportunities,
while those who strive
to fulfill their goals
watch the clock tensely,
never sure when things end.

Abandonment

The voices of the righteous
are raised virtuously
in the halls of government
by our concerned leaders
who always look sincere
when they tell us they care.
These are the same folk
who bailed out the big banks,
the auto companies,
the insurance companies,
without doing anything,
while millions lost jobs, homes,
since they were too small to save.

Policy Failures

The ideals of the republic
handed down for generations
were prepared by men of wealth
who elected custodians
to preserve their privileges,
the exact same policy
since time immemorial
to separate the classes,
maintain the rights of the rich,
keep the people dependent,
superficial values shaped
by Hollywood, television,
so they never interfere
with the owners of power.
The hirelings who serve the system
levy taxes, exempt their masters,
enact laws that protect profits,
while parents lose jobs, homes,
children go hungry,
as the servants of privilege
squander our money
on unwinnable foreign wars.
Our military efforts
failed in Iraq,
failing in Afghanistan,
leaving death and destruction
when our troops depart,
nothing resolved as chaos reigns
on streets no longer patrolled

by American troops
shedding blood far from home,
where their homes are foreclosed
while they're fighting far away
to build democracy
in a theocracy
that hates us passionately,
as does most of the world
oppressed by our capitalists,
secure in their possessions,
since most of us
do not understand
who owns America.

Migration Pattern

The middle class
flocked to Manhattan
to live the cultural life,
more sophisticated
than outer boroughs.
Then rents and prices went up
and they moved to ethnic neighborhoods,
not chic, but affordable,
driving out the locals
who couldn't pay higher rents,
called gentrification,
to delude the gullible
that it was improvement,
rather than displacement
of the unprotected.
When rents went up again,
the middle-class moved
to outer borough neighborhoods,
again driving out the ethnics
and upgrading the area,
at least economically,
artificially creating
cultural enclaves
that weren't very cultural
but comforted the migrants
that they still belonged
to Western civilization.

Danger Zones

Bad news is reported daily
disasters in Africa,
crises in the Middle-East,
recession in Europe,
setbacks in Asia,
so many problems at home
it is hard to imagine
how our beleaguered people
can survive endless threats
and still go shopping.

Burden of Democracy

Too many Americans
feel persecuted
by news reports
warning of dire consequences
if they go to Greece, Africa,
the Middle-East, ride the subway,
go to a movie,
visit a shopping mall
where lunatics are lurking
armed with automatic weapons,
eager to use assault rifles
on targets of opportunity,
deterrence only possible
by odd coincidence,
armed security personnel
prepared for intervention,
the only alternative
to stay at home.

The Lost

The forgotten men
walk city streets
tired, cold, hungry,
options subtracted
leaving corrosive despair,
existence day to day
haphazard coincidence,
desolate victims
rendered inarticulate
in the Information Age,
lost to communication,
trapped in isolation.

Divided Nation

Educated people
join a profession
that rewards efforts
with comfort, security,
even pride in status,
the return for attending
a learning factory.
Some less educated,
but also ambitious,
join the military,
don't open their books,
study rifle 101
learn how to kill,
rather than bookkeeping.
G.I.'s face frequent perils
civilians never encounter,
which sets them apart
from the foreign life back home
grown stranger to them daily,
with increasing rampages
turning the country
into a war zone
with unexpected attacks
not quite often enough,
at least not yet,
to throw us into panic.
When the troops come home,
those who still have a home,
because the banks have been busy

while they were bleeding far away,
flagrantly foreclosing
vulnerable homes,
owners too busy
serving their country
to dispute what they owed.
Yet when banks collapsed
the government rushed
to bail them out,
they were too big to fail,
callously creating
a new doctrine,
a capitalist dogma,
the little are too small
to bother saving.

Redemption

The state of the world
despite civilization,
war, famine, disease, climate change
destroys the lives of millions
threatens the lives of billions,
I lament my lack of power
to relieve suffering, save the lost,
yet somehow I persevere,
try to be of good cheer,
sustained for a moment
watching children at play.

Susceptible

I'm too tired to work,
so I turn on the tv
that tries to submerge me
into channels of response,
instructions to buy something
whether I need it or not,
graphic demonstrations
with painstaking details
of every type of crime
actually committed,
or created by writers,
motivation day or night
to get up from the couch,
grab my assault rifle,
go out and kill someone,
courtesy of the sponsors
whose inspiring messages
saturate the airways,
eroding repugnance
for iniquitous acts.

Deeds, Not Words

So many of us
believe in the afterlife,
encouraged by religion
with fervent promises
of forgiveness, atonement
for what we did wrong
designed to console us
for failures, unhappiness
in this intolerant life,
making some of us wonder
why it's insufficient
to be good, do right
in daily existence.

Democracy in Action

The streets are filled
with forgotten men and women,
poor, desperate, homeless,
while the lords of profit
feast in their mansions
unconcerned with the well-being
of fellow citizens
ignored by secure congressmen,
who will shut down the government
at the behest of their masters,
rather than do their duty
for the suffering people.

Innovative

We acquire habits
depending on class, wealth,
education, inclination,
some good, some bad.
For those who read books
many elders remember
when books had hard covers.
Then paperbacks spread quickly
and it was good for the people,
reading accessible to all
at a reasonable price.
E books snuck up on us
and it didn't take long
till they had their own listing
on the bestseller list,
although some people
could not accept
not turning the pages.

Measurements

Babies swaddled by Mammas
before they go outside,
infants carefully dressed,
youngsters dress themselves,
teens grab wallet, keys, jacket,
men put on shirts, ties, suits,
seniors prepare carefully
checklist by Boeing,
something always forgotten,
irksome lapse of memory
defers destination
for further preparation.

Dire Event

First responders to disaster
rush into danger
regardless of risk
to save the imperiled.
Second responders
reach out to the victims
with medical aid,
food, shelter, clothing.
Politicians promise
improved response next time,
financial aid for losses
that never happen fast enough
to relieve the suffering
of those in need.

Banners

The meeting of true minds
is a social rarity
and like all good encounters,
whether destiny, coincidence,
must be carefully nurtured,
since it is difficult
to leave the confines of our minds
separated by suspicion
and reach out to another,
making us reluctant
to reveal ourselves.

Expedition

Tourists flock to America
while the exchange rate is favorable,
buying what they can't afford at home,
flaunting their prosperity
in front of the natives
of a depressed economy,
who don't have money to buy
name brands, designer labels,
and can only watch with envy
as foreigners who hate us,
except for Hollywood films,
coca cola, Andy Warhol,
acquire everything in sight,
leaving our hospitable shores
having looted treasures
from the new world.

Slow Change

The first day
of the new year
feels no different
than the last day
of the old year,
except my brain
may be fractionally tireder,
my body composition
losing atoms faster,
my learning process
in the Information Age
definitely slower,
only my feeble hope
rheumatically endures
that I will gain a little wisdom
before my lease expires.

Thoughts

I do not know
when death will come
because I cannot see
the final moment
before eternity.

Let those I love
not mourn for me
for I received more
than I hoped for.

A few will miss me
I hope not for long,
since I cannot help them
as they go on.

Santa Convention

Shortly before christmas
hundreds of celebrants
dress in Santa suits
and go from bar to bar
drinking, socializing,
most having a good time,
too many falling down drunk,
puking their guts on the street,
passing out in doorways,
collapsing on the sidewalks
for children to see
the squalor of Santa.

Lost Soul

We stagger through life
without purpose, plan,
lurching forward
haphazard as the storm
devoured by wanting,
unable to control
wrathful appetite,
devoid of service
to a greater cause,
still trapped in worship
of the golden calf.

Purchase Prod

Somehow
without conscious choice
we have succumbed
to giving gifts
for the sake of gifts.
Parents run to buy
dolls, video games, action figures,
without considering
if there should be
other priorities,
as the temples of acquisition
chant, buy, buy, buy,
spend, spend, spend,
regardless
of what we can afford.

Condition Normal

Across our troubled land
more and more disasters strike,
some wreaked on us by nature
unbalanced by the works of man,
more and more destructive acts
killing children, the elderly,
tragically unprotected
since we can't watch over all,
increasing rampage incidents
targeting schools, malls, movie theaters,
most frequently the workplace
where the disaffected return
armed, detached, implacable,
ruthlessly performing better
than any previous function,
murdering methodically,
finally killing themselves
after destroying the lives of others
in untimely slaughter,
frequently inexplicable
when breaking upon strangers,
leaving the gift of mourning
for devastated survivors
who cannot comprehend
the death by murder
of precious loved ones.

A Toast

I watch the old year wind down
from the comfort of my living room,
color tv showing the crowd
cold but cheerful, exhilarated,
waving for the cameras.
I sit on the couch,
champagne glass in hand,
sipping the minutes away
until the count by celebrants
tells me the old year is over,
although I feel no different.

Poor Choices

The yells of approval
for football games
resound in packed stadiums,
while the empty corridors
of math and science buildings
are hauntingly silent.

Fair Share

I lost my job
in the recession,
lost my home
when I couldn't pay the mortgage.
Now my family lives
in a homeless shelter.
We don't eat too well,
while the lords of profit,
bailed out by the government,
stuff themselves on caviar.

Streamlining

We persist in life
driven by hungers,
eager to acquire
wealth, power, fame,
public acclaim
for service to the state,
achievement of desires.
Yet as we rush to the end
some of us realize
we can't take anything with us,
so the wise want less and less,
shedding burdens of possessions
as we prepare for whatever
does or does not come next.

Nourishment

When the evil of the world
seems to possess my soul
I relieve some of my anguish
looking at a Christmas cactus,
exquisite red-pink blossoms
bursting with beauty,
and for a few peaceful heartbeats
I am reenergized,
resume the tribulations,
as well as redeeming joys
encouraging continuation.

Reminder

Bursts of passion,
more infrequent as we age,
arouse ardent desire,
reminding some of us
we're still fortunate
to have a lover.

Acts of Madness

 A crazed man
stormed into a school,
shooting anyone who moved,
able to keep firing
courtesy of
automatic weapon,
dramatically demonstrating
adaptability
to civilian targets,
increasingly vulnerable
in an insane society
that allows the gun industry
to fully equip lunatics
for unregulated slaughter.

Ode to Labor

There is no song
for millions of toilers
who work each day,
keep the nation running,
never know splendors,
deprived or ignored
by the privileged,
not appreciated
by most of us,
forgetful,
dazed by realities,
dazzled by the wealthy,
until we do not know
how to say thank you
for the ongoing efforts
that make things function.

Another End of Days

Today,
December 21, 2012,
according to an ancient Mayan calendar
the world will end,
at least according to some
who obviously
have nothing better to do
then worry about old predictions,
repeated many times in the past,
mostly, coincidentally,
by crumbling civilizations
possibly trying to spite
surviving cultures,
reminding us
primitive genes
still possess our minds.

Carpe Diem

Valuable gifts
often are unappreciated
by those too busy
to stop and look
at delicate flowers,
a glorious sunset,
the elegant works of man,
the ugly works of man
outnumbering by far
inspired creations,
the spectacle of life
savored by the senses,
too briefly for some,
as time rushes us away.

Simulacra

Cities share the same needs
transportation to work, to play,
to visit friends, family,
dispose of waste,
human and other,
since the nineteenth century
electricity
to power lights, everything
that modern man
is dependant on,
houses, regardless of style,
the only difference
the language barrier,
keeping us estranged.

Aftermath

Indicators of disturbance
are rarely noted
before a violent rampage,
and the few exceptions
are rarely treated.
But after the eruption,
experts tell us
what we should have done,
the media shows us
suffering for lost loved ones,
everyone solemn, sincere,
totally unprepared
for the next disaster.

Destabilization

Crime, like other enactments
bursts upon the innocent
shocking in the sudden assault
on sensibilities focused elsewhere,
earning a living, visiting friends,
unprepared for the threat, loss,
disrupting industrious lives
never expecting they will be
victims of illicit acts.

Spirit of Acquisition

Shoppers rush to stores,
line up three days early
avid for the newest gadget,
unable to recognize
the waste of living time
waiting for a desired device
reveals their poverty.

Buyers cruise the Internet
urgent for special deals
electronically removed
from human transactions
allaying normal suspicions
of purchase conditions,
placing trust in electrons.

False Alarm

Screams pierce the urban night,
first reaction, call the police,
rush to help those in danger,
then sudden peal of laughter
eases the tension
calming adrenalin rush,
when the perilous alarm
is only people having fun.

Illusory Image

Our leaders,
nurtured by tv,
wear slick suits,
slicker faces
to get elected,
as qualified
as average household pets
to run a complex nation.
Somehow, sincere looks,
concerned statements,
convince many of us
unqualified politicians
can be trusted
to solve our problems.

Farewell

I do not know
when I pass on
if I will miss
nuclear sunsets,
Beethoven,
my loved ones,
since what comes next
is unknown to me.
I'll leave with no regrets,
having given up
most of my desire
for material things,
my remaining hope
before departure
the good I have done
will not dissipate.

Eruption

Gunfire echoes
across a troubled land.
It is not the Congo,
Afghanistan, Chechnya,
but the good old U.S.A.,
where disturbed young men
with automatic weapons
slaughter the innocent
in insane rampages
for a moment's attention
before self-destruction,
followed by analysis
courtesy of the media,
glibly explaining everything
until the next hot news item
breeds instant forgetfulness.

Information Gap

The world turns faster
since the internet
and although we may be
more communicative,
we are still not connected,
as war, crime, terrorism,
continues unabated
and the people are helpless,
as the people always have been,
to stop the violence
that consumes our lives.

Revel

The new year approaches,
celebration for planting
completely neglected
in a meaningless party
that reaches its apex
in the drunken counting out
of the quickly forgotten
previous year.

Beyond Comfort

A madman went on a rampage
possessed by calculating rage
and slaughtered innocent children.
It makes no difference to us
when experts explain why,
the precious children are still lost.

Aggravated by his neighbor
an angry tenant set a fire
and burned two families to death.
It doesn't change anything
if we're told his motives,
two families went up in flames.

In a land of lunacy,
we can't stop drunken drivers
from killing thousands,
and gun-nuts loudly claim
second amendment rights
to own automatic weapons,
where child molesters and rapists
are conserved in prisons,
though why any society
wants to keep such monsters
eludes intelligent answers.

In a land swept by violence
citizens lose jobs, homes,
are neglected by congress

elected to serve the people,
but hired to obey their masters
and guard the portals of the wealthy.
There is little hope for change,
unless the rich and powerful
renounce selfish interests
and rescue a failing nation,
an unlikely occurrence,
since their mega-yachts
are ready to set sail.

Thwarted Shoppers

The prosperous course the streets
purchasing tantalizing goods
from beckoning shops
promising satisfaction
with extravagant treasures
denied ordinary folk,
who can no longer afford
to buy what they want,
rudely reduced
to second-class consumers.

Unreconciled

It's only been a few days,
but New Year's resolutions
already forgotten
in recurrence of routine,
the normal pattern
for most Americans
struggling to survive
loss of prosperity,
diminished opportunity,
previous expectations
aggravated
by passing limousines.

The Way

The fight for life,
        primal,
constant,
            relentless,
goes on everywhere,
but humans
        preoccupied
with important affairs,
don't notice
daily struggles
        of other creatures,
striving,
   failing,
       dying,
   unmourned,
nothing learned
     about the natural way.

Narrow is the Gate

America the cruel
allows children
to grow without love,
guidance, protection,
dispensable
in a harsh society
that only has room
for select offspring
of prosperity.

Viewer's Choice

Those who can afford tickets
to the theater, opera,
savoring the culture
of a city of prosperity,
where millions skimp on meals,
worry about their children
denied opportunity
because of poverty,
tormented daily by tv
flaunting glamorous lives
of those who have everything
that entertains the deprived,
who must constantly resist
feelings of hate and envy,
which would consume them.

Price Tag

Shoppers spend
on the unnecessary,
clogging their lives
with weighty accumulations
of goods of little value,
completely unaware
they are what they purchase.

Bulletin Board

Each morning on the news
we hear another threat,
currently schools
the victims
of dissatisfied students
eager to pay back
the system that warped them.
We are now acclimatized
to lunatics attacking
malls, the workplace, movie houses,
low or middle-income targets,
while righteous legislators call
for stricter gun control laws
to keep automatic weapons
out of the hands of the disturbed,
who somehow always get their hands
on automatic weapons,
despite legal restrictions
constantly challenged by gun-nuts,
who claim they need assault rifles
to eliminate garden pests,
dangerous gophers, woodchucks.
So stronger laws will be passed
without serious objections
from not-for-profit gun lobbies
confident that gun customers
will find ways to make purchases
and keep the profits growing.
Circumstances may change

if the insane rampagers
select new targets,
museums, expensive restaurants,
theaters, the opera house,
cultural institutions
supported by wealthy patrons,
mansions where the rich reside
suddenly vulnerable
to unexpected assault.
This will motivate the privileged
to take immediate action
to prevent bloody disruptions
of their comfortable lives.

Interference

Insufficient oxygen
impeded by toxins
stupefies my system
blurring my consciousness,
launching waves of fatigue
that drain my concentration,
restricting functioning
preventing completion
of designated tasks.

Flu

Illness is as seasonal
as baseball or football,
with a growing tempo,
spreading across the country,
affecting more and more of us,
infecting more and more of us,
sneezing, coughing, sniffling,
bodies burning with fever,
muscles aching, bones brittle,
just managing to digest
a little bit of broth,
brain remains in idle
barely able to concentrate,
a capsule of inertia
recuperation uncertain.
Some use pharmaceuticals,
some supplement with religion,
hoping that illness
will runs its course.

Cultural Preferences

The roar of the crowd
for a rock concert,
sporting event, fight,
quite drives out the sounds
of bird song, gentle waves,
classical music,
less confrontational
than strident yells
for crude entertainment.

Pleasure Trip

Tourists rush to America
encouraged by the exchange rate,
the buying power of the Euro.
They flock to museums, theaters,
devouring cultural events
never attended at home,
only after shopping is done
treasures obtained
as income allows,
then going home,
acquisition appetites,
sufficiently nourished.

.

Contagion

Children went to school one day
some happy, some afraid,
most hoping to learn,
then a madman attacked
murdering innocents.
For a short while
we were horrified,
and most of us approved
demands for gun control.
Clever politicians
eager for advancement
seemed to support the public
and listened to their demands.
But soon the media
moved on to other news
and attention faded,
so nothing was done
to treat a disease
sweeping America,
a plague of violence
occurring so often
that a possible cure
might be a vaccine
that builds antibodies
to resist extreme rage.
Another option
might be a device
to detect the disturbed
before they detonate.

In any event,
disease control is needed
more than gun control.

Chill Out

The day before the first freeze
city dwellers mostly sheltered
by urban comforts,
ignore changing conditions
considering the weather
an inconvenience
to normal routines,
only interrupted
by occasional storms, snow,
paralyzing blackout,
frigid temperatures
an opportunity
for displays of finery
by the fashion conscious,
a reason for complaint
from the disaffected,
all forgetting discomfort
when warm winds start to blow.

Lack of Compassion

Months after the storm
people still huddle in darkness
frigid days and nights
chilling the life from them,
as government agencies,
concerned organizations,
find feeble explanations
for bureaucratic delays
that do not consider
the suffering of the people.

Urban Oddity

Time and again
a store or restaurant
opens for business
near a store or restaurant
that sells the exact same thing.
Survival depends
on customer loyalty,
convenience, better service,
more appealing product,
all the tangibles
that allow success
in a trade war
that no one understands
why it happened
on the same street.

Obedience Training

Presidential proclamations
fall on deaf ears in Congress
where special interests supplant
agendas that help the needy.
Many ignorant voters
never seem to understand
the purchaser's of legislators
expect them to do as ordered,
regardless of any harm
to the American people.

Random Harvest

What we do each day
creates a structure
that shapes existence.
Most try to subsist,
some pursue power,
many yearn for wealth
stretching the boundaries
of what they'll do for gain,
while some snap from frustration,
lack of appreciation,
go on a bloody rampage
slaughtering the innocent,
because they did not get
what they wanted.

Assessment

Despite the ravages of time
illness, disease,
I still maintain some function
and if I produce
creative work of worth
I shall endure,
regardless of discomfort,
decreasing abilities,
as long as
I demonstrate
redeeming value.

Viewing Pleasure

We seek the pleasures of the world
encouraged daily by tv
to commit rape, drink while driving,
use drugs, carry out murders
gorier in reality
than those sanitized on tv
that soften the lurid impact
of battered bodies, bloody wounds,
to spare the sensibilities
of impressionable viewers
who might react to what we're shown,
conclude it's government approved
because when we turn on the tv
we always see violence, crime,
all the other vicious actions
we can possibly imagine,
eroding our morality,
by entertaining us with evil.

Shallow Thinking

Some of us think,
especially doctors,
that making comparisons
between us and someone else,
often for health issues,
telling us we're better off
than almost everyone else,
we'll be consoled
others are worse off.

Auld Lang Syne

Each New Year's Eve
celebrants gather
in Times Square
cordoned into small groups
for public safety,
some waiting hour after hour
for the ball to drop
ushering in another year
that may or may not be better
than the one peacefully ended,
as guardians of the state
heave a sigh of relief
that there were no disasters.

Configured Values

The spirit of Christmas
is measured in dollars
for so many people
that the nature of giving
has been crassly transformed
into ostentatious display
of expensive presents,
instilling children
with material values.

Tested

Across our conflicted land
evil dominates the news
twisting the minds of people
until pessimism prevails,
the good often unnoticed.
Sometimes we give in to despair
when overwhelmed by problems.
Then we must renew strength
to continue our best efforts
to master weaknesses
that prevent better functioning,
interfere with doing good.

Yule

The city gears up
for Christmas holiday,
hundreds of santas
going from bar to bar
drinking seasons greetings,
 bartenders eager to welcome
merrymakers
with excess of alcohol
in the time of giving.

Vacation

Tourists course the streets
cameras clicking urgently
at anything of attraction,
buildings, signs, people,
rushing through museums
taking photos of paintings
instead of looking,
experiencing their trip
with vicarious efforts
to accumulate pictures
to show the folks at home,
able to share the same
indirect pleasures.

Errant Lust

Desire often leads to lust
for the body of another,
material possessions,
accumulation of more
regardless of basic need,
the process of acquisition
become more important
than enjoyment of the moment.

Shattered Stillness

Shoppers crowd city streets
burdened with packages
jostling each other
on Fifth Avenue,
where they push and shove
to get a closer look
at the Christmas tree
in Rockefeller Center,
ornate symbol
of what we lack,
peace on earth,
good will to men.

Lunacy Quatrain

Children went to school one day
for the usual work and play
but a madman shattered their class
with rampage, the American way.

Imbalance

To some the measure of wealth
is in vast estates, mega-yachts,
Picasso and Warhol paintings,
precious material things,
possessions that define owners
in the envious eyes of others.

Then there are the less avaricious
uneager to accumulate
more than they appreciate,
concerned with what they truly want,
not deluded into desiring
artificial values of others.

The voracity of the wealthy
is not counterbalanced by those
who do not require approval
in the scornful eyes of others,
the oppressions of excessive wealth
afflicting the less well off.

Old Acquaintance

Revelers flock to Times Square
tourists, locals, the homeless,
eager to welcome the new year,
many doing without liquor, drugs,
courtesy of attentive police
at best barely tolerated,
until joy of celebration
is rudely interrupted
by sudden terrorist threat.

Resist Decline

Again and again
in this brutal land
shots ring out
killing the innocent
and in the aftermath
all we hear is talk.

The self-righteous call
for a ban on guns,
psychologists analyze,
the media explain,
politicians promise,
but nothing changes.

Our violent culture,
numbed by video games,
glossy movies, constant tv,
erupts frequently
in mindless destruction,
fists, knives, assault rifles,
and we still haven't learned
that automatic weapons
are used for mass murder,
not deer hunting.

All our efforts will fail
to prevent mad rampages
until we change the culture
that approves constant exposure

to every kind of violence
permeating the mindsets
of our citizens,
young and old.

In our decaying system
family values dissolve
from the stress of daily burdens,
or insufficient caring,
leaving the only hope
for a safer society
in revolutionary change.

Our failing schools
should face the issues
blighting our nation,
instruct our children
to compete fairly,
appreciate effort,
resolve conflicts without fighting,
prepare them to understand
why a society allows
destructive drug use
enriching criminals,
why almost all our entertainment
promotes violence,
why there is no moral instruction.

If our nation hopes to endure
we must change the environment
that educates our children,
find willing teachers
who will fight to preserve our children,

prepare them for the future struggle
to preserve hope
of the American dream.

Faint Resolve

The old year's revels ended
replaced by a grey, chilled day,
celebrants of the night before
groggy from too much champagne,
slowly stir and go their way,
some sincere resolutions
already quite forgotten,
others in imminent danger
of formal renunciation,
since the pledge before drunkenness
is surely less substantial
than a clear-headed decision
to aspire to be better.

Ritual Proceedings

Millions of voters
are given the choice
of who to vote for
on election day,
which makes Americans proud
of their democracy,
even though candidates
are selected and purchased
by special interests,
more concerned with profits
than the needs of the people.

Darkening Days

Disease spreads across the land.
The media tell us loudly
that it's never been this bad,
as more and more are dying.
Not long ago a major storm
ravaged the Northeast.
The media told us loudly
that it never was this bad,
with many deaths,
widespread destruction.
Madmen rampage through our schools.
The media tells us loudly
that it's never been this bad,
with microscopic coverage
as cameras persecute
bereaved families.
Extreme disasters increase.
The media tells us loudly
that it's never been this bad,
but no one seems to speculate
they all may be connected.

Vista

Throughout history
cataclysmic occurrences
swept us away,
the loss of control
no consolation
for pain and suffering
we did or did not deserve,
innocent and guilty alike
rendered helpless
by overwhelming events.

I.D. Tags

Shoppers proudly wear
brand name clothes,
carry famous label bags,
proclaiming to the world
their secure place
in consumer land.

Conjectures

The ancient Greeks
at least the literate,
were concerned with philosophy,
ethics and morality,
attempting to understand
the confusing universe,
offering various answers
some fanciful, some sensible,
none really resolving
earthly problems.

Preferences

The first winter chill
assaults the city
catching many unprepared
for freezing temperature,
dressing stylishly,
unwilling to be seen
in unfashionable clothes,
preferring to be cold,
as long as they look good.

Resigned

We are the deceived,
the deluded,
who believe what we're told,
except cynics, criminals,
suspicious enough to know
the owners of our land
do not care for the people,
unless they need the people,
who are unfairly burdened
as the poor, the voiceless,
those who can't purchase protection
against official oppression,
let alone violent gangsters,
are always compelled to accept
infliction from the heartless,
never sufficient recourse
to change the nature of man.

Sales Pitch

Parents take children
to a hi-tech conference
sponsored for a day of learning
by an electronics giant,
seemingly benevolent,
but planning to sell
the latest equipment
to the next generation.

Uneven Rule

In a conflicted country
citizens struggle daily
to endure the next disaster,
domestic or foreign.
Long term grievances fester
prompting protests, or indifference.
People refuse to reconcile
their beliefs with others.
Crises erupt suddenly
shattering the tranquility
of those who think their lives secure,
oblivious to reality
that existence is coincidence,
stability an illusion
fostered by the lords of profit,
more sheltered from disruption
by the shield of wealth
when calamity strikes,
leaving the less fortunate
to bear the brunt of suffering.

Missions

Prosperous America
at least for the select,
is a complex state
with a vast variety
of endless problems,
and we are fortunate
to have dedicated people,
despite disloyal opposition,
who give their best
to resolve difficulties,
regardless of importance,
to improve conditions
for those of us unable
to advocate for ourselves.

The Big Picture

Our leaders must know
that extreme storms,
erratic weather patterns,
diminishing rain and snow
indicate climate change
that will alter our lives,
endanger existence,
threaten calamity,
yet they can't agree
on a national budget,
seem to be willing
to shut down the government
devastating many lives
rather than compromise,
let alone take action
to save our imperiled land.

Medical Emergency

Dangerous diseases
afflict our country
eroding our system,
the body politic
weakening daily
from such dissension,
we no longer know
who can be trusted
to guide us safely
in perilous times.

Torch of Freedom

In the age of democracy
persecuted people
turn to their government
for relief from suffering,
and often discover
the government doesn't care.
Then persecuted people
turn to family, friends, neighbors,
to help resist oppression.
If they don't face armed forces
they have a chance for redress.
If their government is strong
and uses its military
to suppress insurrection,
the results will be bloody
and protesters usually lose.
When abusers are local
and people unite
they may overcome oppressors
and reestablish justice.

Poems from Redemption Value have appeared in

A New Ulster, A Quiet Courage, Amsterdam Quarterly, Ancient Heart Magazine, BlogNostics, Boston Accent Lit, Cabildo Quarterly, Carcinogenic Poetry (Virgogray Press), Pyrokinection (Kind of a Hurricane Press), Joey and the Black Boot (kitty Litter Press), Locust Press, Madness Muse Press, mgversion2datura, Midnight Circus (EAB Publishing), Millers Pond Poetry Magazine (H&H Press), Pilcrow & Dagger, Poetic Diversity, Purplepig Lit. Scarlet Leaf Review, The Broadkill Review, The Homestead Review, The Pen/The Poetry Band (The Poetry, Explosion Newsletter), The Write Place At The Right Time, University of Puget Sound's Collins Memorial Library, Vita Brevis, Winamop Magazine, WINK: Writers in the Know, Work Literary Magazine, Writer's Block Magazine, Ygdrasil Journal